Turd Ferguson
&
the Sausage Party

Turd Ferguson & the Sausage Party

◆

An Uncensored Guide to College Slang

Compiled by
Ben Applebaum and Derrick Pittman

Illustrations by Burt Falgui
Cover Design by Donald J. Mock

iUniverse, Inc.
New York Lincoln Shanghai

Turd Ferguson & the Sausage Party
An Uncensored Guide to College Slang

iUniverse, Inc.

For information address:
iUniverse, Inc.
2021 Pine Lake Road, Suite 100
Lincoln, NE 68512
www.iuniverse.com

ISBN: 0-595-30923-2

Printed in the United States of America

Dedicated to our families for their support—especially Val, Mike, Jackie, and Maggie.

"All slang is metaphor, and all metaphor is poetry."
—G. K. Chesterton

**"Slang is a language that rolls up its sleeves,
spits on its hands and goes to work."**
—Carl Sandburg

"I speak fluent Jive."
—Elderly woman in the movie "Airplane"

Contents

PREFACE. xi

A words. 1

B words. 4

C words 11

D words 15

E words. 19

F words. 20

G words 25

H words 28

I words 32

J words 34

K words. 38

L words 41

M words 43

N words 47

O words 48

P words. 50

Q words 56

R words. 57

S words 60

T words 64

U words 70

V words 71

W words 73

Y words 76

Z words 77

AFTERWORD 79

ABOUT THE AUTHORS 81

SHOUT-OUTS 83

PREFACE

WHO THE? WHAT THE?

It's one thing to walk the college-student walk: dress in dirty clothes, sleep during the day, and occasionally study. But it's another thing to talk the college-student talk. Would you rather be a *sonny* or a *wedge*? Does a *turkey dump* have anything to do with *taking the kids to the pool*? And most importantly, who's *Turd Ferguson* and what's he doing at *a sausage party*?

Fear not, Skippy. We're here to help. We're the editors of CollegeStories.com—a website for undergrads and postgrads to share their favorite college memories. In 1999, we started emailing stories back and forth with our fellow recent graduates. One day we thought maybe other kids would be interested in reading and sharing their favorite tales too. So we made a website.

Now every day thousands of college students and grads waste valuable time on our site—reliving their glory days and giving lots of good advice. *Entertainment Weekly* calls our site "a queasy mix of Girls Gone Wild and the Ken Starr report." And who are we to argue?

CollegeStories.com has received a lot of attention over the past 4 years. We get submissions from people all over the globe. And after reading over 2,000 college memories, we have become pretty well versed in the goings-on of campus life (and the drinking practices of Australian rugby players). Along the way, we've also picked up a few insider terms. And now we've compiled a few hundred of them to share with you in this book. How about them apples?

WHY THE SLANG

Intellectuals often disregard slang as improper and ignorant. Well, those skeezers ain't got nothing up in their domes, fo' sheezy.

Slang is actually a fascinating natural process—like monkeys mating. Pamela Munro, professor and author of *Slang U.*, defines slang as "language whose use serves to mark the user as a part of a distinct social group."

So like a secret handshake, slang keeps those in the know in, and those out of it out. And when you are in college—stuck between high school youngsters and

xi

working-world stiffs—you find yourselves bonding in a pretty serious way. Thus, college slang develops.

By looking at the slang on college campuses you get some insight into college life and relationships. So this book is not just about funny terms, it's a little slice of the best years of your life. And all of this through a bunch of funny, stupid terms. Who'd have thunk it?

HOW WE PICKED THE WINNERS

As you can imagine, we received many, many submissions. And we've read many, many of them. Some stunk. But some stuck, and we'd like to share those good ones with you. To decide which terms made the cut, we used our patent-pending five "U" criteria:

1. Unique to college. College students pull from many sources. Not surprisingly, much of college slang comes from different arenas—like hip-hop, for example. But we wanted to keep the book focused on slang that is more exclusive to the campus quad than to the hood.

2. Universal usage. Every group of friends has funny terms they bat around. These are great, but we didn't think Kwan in California would care that Allen in Georgia calls Barry's car "the hoagie." So we looked for words that seem to be used by a larger group—even if they are more regional than international.

3. Underlying truths. We tried to find words that speak to the reality of college. It's not all about academic enlightenment. You are living, sleeping and sharing a toilet with more people than you ever will in your life. A lot of talk revolves around some pretty base subjects: drinking, humping and eating. Sorry moms and dads, but that's the truth about tuition.

4. Understanding for us to share. We know that many of our readers will be incoming freshmen, nervous about the big transition. We've been through it. And we've heard from hundreds of others who have too. So throughout the book, we've tried to add little nuggets of advice. Just consider it a little help from the big brothers you never knew.

5. Underpants. We needed another "U" word. But it's also a reminder to take everything with a large grain of salt. Even a ham-sized hunk of salt, if you wish.

For example, we don't condone illegal drug use, excessive drinking, irresponsible behavior, objectifying women or training squirrels to fight in "American Gladiators" outfits. But some of the terms do touch on these behaviors.

Also remember that knowing the terminology might actually help you (or your kid) avoid bad situations. If you know what *hot boxing* is then maybe you can leave the room before the joints get passed about. So this book might actually keep you safe and adjusted. Chew on that.

WHAT YOU'LL SEE

If you are still reading this introduction, you're a saint—a saint that wants to get moving on to the good stuff. So, without further ado, here's the different stuff you'll find on the following pages:

Mucho terms. We're talking about hundreds, so enjoy. They are conveniently organized in alphabetical order and unsanitized for your pleasure.

Advice. Like we said above, it's our way of sharing some of our learnin' with you. But don't hold us to anything.

Memories. The book is also peppered with real memories from real students. These are original tales told to us on CollegeStories.com. You can't find these anywhere else in the world. But don't worry, we don't charge extra for this much extra fun.

Unlike the crop of other "official college slang dictionaries" out there, we haven't set out to catalog the etymology of campus dialects. No sir. Who needs another reference aid? Not us. We simply want our book to be an amusing read, chock full of silly nuggets. If you are looking for a quick way to locate the next "dope" or "fly", you won't find it here.

But what you will find is a great way to prepare for college life—or just remember it. It's a great little conversation piece for a coffee table or a daily giggle for your special time on the can. Read it cover to cover, or hop around. Share it with friends or stash it in your undies drawer so your parents don't find it. We don't care. We just hope you'll be able to speak fluent college slang in no time.

Cheers!

Ben and Derrick

A

A

A letter grade you might have been used to in high school but will rarely see in college.

ACA

Short for Acute Commitment Anxiety. A common disorder in young collegiate students who suffer from an extreme fear of relationships. Often fuels chronic one-night stands and early-morning getaways.

Antiqued

When someone passes out or falls asleep early; you coat them with handfuls of flour—making them look old and dusty.

Ape Shit

To lose control for any number of reasons.

When he found out someone peed on his bed, Barry went ape shit and fixed the bunk beds and dressers.

Around the World

A party theme during which participants move through different rooms, each decorated in a theme of a different country with the appropriate alcoholic beverages provided.

Ladies, you should stop by our Around the World party. My room is Guam.

Art Fag

Someone really involved with the school's art scene. Usually has thick-rimmed glasses and listens to cryptic, dark music. Doesn't refer to sexual preference.

Ape Shit

Asshole

A simple, yet popular, drinking game that involves a hierarchy of players from president to asshole. Played with a deck of cards for hours and often ends up with very silly rules, which also makes it a fun spectator sport.

Ass Hug

Cuddling all night with someone. Though innocent, the act looks more salacious when your roommate accidentally walks in on you and is all, "Sorry, I didn't know you two were going at it." And you're all, "Whatever, beeotch." Also known as **Spooning** and **Fancy Sleeping**.

ATM Bomb

Withdrawing too much cash from the money tree, thereby obliterating your bank account.

Atomic Sit-up

A prank in which a bunch of guys convinces a chump that he can't complete this "ultimate test of strength." Long story short: the chump's face ends up in the butt crack of one of the perpetrators.

B

Bad Idea Jeans

When one behaves in a most idiotic fashion. Derived from an "SNL" skit in the mid '90s.

The guy trying to touch that cop's gun is wearing Bad Idea Jeans.

REAL COLLEGE MEMORY:
"Bad Idea Roof Launching"

No matter how hard I tried, I just couldn't get along with my freshman-year roommate, so I always stayed at this girl Michelle's room. One night we were both sleeping when her boyfriend called and asked us to come over to his frat house. We dragged our tired asses all the way across campus to find the whole house eerily empty—except her boyfriend Jeff and his two friends, Chris and Ed. They were all drinking already so we joined them, and pretty soon we were all completely waxed.

Chris decided to drag Ed and Jeff's mattresses outside and lay them in the backyard so we could have something to sit on. We just laid there talking about something stupid and, out of nowhere, Chris turned to me and said, "Wanna see how good these mattresses really are?" Thinking that he was pressuring me into a sick sexual thing, I started to get up and walk away. That's when he stood up and explained to me what he wanted to do: "C'mon, let's go jump off the roof and onto the mattresses." The building was **only** two stories and I was feeling good (and relieved he wasn't trying to sleep with me), so I was like, "Sure!"

We tied sheets around our necks and stole this huge umbrella—marching through the house like disabled superheroes. We asked everyone else to go outside with a camera. Chris said he'd go first. He ran up to the edge, opened the umbrella, and leapt off. I was laughing so hard I could barely breathe. But without waiting to see if Chris survived, I tightened my bed-sheet cape and took the twenty-foot plunge. I hit the mattress with a solid thud. It hurt a little, but the effects of the alcohol magically took away most of the pain. Soon Ed joined in, and he introduced the requirement that after every jump, we would take a shot. After about five jumps (and shots), Ed jumped again, and after he landed I heard a big commotion down below.

I didn't care.

The second I saw him move; I jumped off the roof with my arms and legs flailing away. I soared through the night sky—free from the limitations of gravity and sobriety. When I hit the mattress, man, was I in for a surprise. I learned first-hand what all the commotion had been about. Ed had puked all over the mattress after his most recent landing. When my body hit the puddle, puke flew up in my face and into my nose and mouth. I was completely grossed out. I ran around the corner and just started tossing my cookies. I couldn't even shower because as soon as I was done throwing up, I promptly passed out in the grass.

I haven't gone "Roof Launching" since that night, but the guys continue to wear bad idea jeans and still do it all the time. But I will never propel myself from that roof again. At least not anytime soon.

—University of Rochester

Bag

To leave a place or skip an event. Also known as **Bolt, Bounce, Bust, Dip,** and **Shine**.

I had a final the next day, so I bagged around 2:00AM.

Baja

Off the beaten path.

Instead of just following the sidewalk, Barry went Baja and ended up losing his pants somewhere in the woods.

Bar Scar

All the wristbands and ink left over after making the rounds at the bars. Also known as **War Wounds**.

By the look of those bar scars, you must have had a good night.

Barking Spiders

Farts.

Batten the Hatches

The act of locking the door and placing a towel under it before toking in your dorm room. Also known as **Lock 'n Towel** and **Lockdown.**

[Advice: Not looking to inhale copious amounts of secondhand reefer smoke? Leave the room before the door gets locked up like this. Once the hatches are battened, you're stuck, Skippy.]

BBD's

Short for Bigger Better Deals. In other words: Leaving a party to go out and find a hotter someone, a better more rocking party, or a cheaper all-night buffet.

BBH

Short for Bros Before Hoes. Which means you're more loyal to your buds than you are to your girlfriend. The opposite is **Chicks Before Dicks.** The female equivalent is **Holes Before Poles.**

Beeracle

A miracle that is caused by almighty beer. For example, someone making ten straight cups in a game of Beirut.

Beer Bitch

The person sitting closest to the cooler or refrigerator at a party whose job it is to grab another beer when yours runs out.

Beer Goggles

One's perception when under the influence of alcohol. Often causes unattractive people to look hot, long distances to look jumpable, and break dancing moves to look easy.

Beer Muscles

A sudden increase in courage and combative abilities directly linked to alcohol consumption.

Barry must have had some beer muscles when he head-butted the bouncer's fist.

Beer Pong

A game played on a ping-pong table in which cups of beer are set at each end. The object is to throw a ping-pong ball into the opponent's cup and then make them drink it. **Beirut** is a popular variation that involves more cups, more balls, and more bruising.

REAL COLLEGE MEMORY:
"The Beer Pong Protégée"

Two years ago as a sophomore, I introduced my freshman friend, Ellen, to beer pong. At first I thought her incredible skill was just beginner's luck, but I now know that this girl is simply a natural.

One night, we showed up at a house party when not much else was going on. We didn't know the people who lived there, but beer is beer, and we were on it. The party was completely lame, so we, naturally, began suggesting that someone set up beer pong. After a bit, we were in full swing and playing the guy who owned the house. So we set up the table for him and his partner, and immediately he was trying to change the rules. I vocalized my unhappiness with his "ghetto-ass rules."

In retrospect, I was a mouthy sophomore girl, who he didn't know and who was drinking his beer. But, this didn't cross my mind at the time, of course. So I continued to insist—loudly—that we were gonna kick his ass, even WITH his shady rules.

Long story short: We were down to one cup each, and he sank the shot first, and even though he tried to stop us from getting our rebuttal shot, everyone in the room disagreed. So we took our final shot. And I hit it. Thus we went into triple cup overtime, and I started making jokes about him losing to girls.

On our last shot, quiet Ellen made the proclamation, "Mary, I'm too drunk; I can't even see the f*cking cups." The crowd hushed. But with a dramatic spin, she turned around and proceeded to sink the winning shot. We flashed him a smile and a "told you so," and went to leave. He was fuming.

One thing led to another, and I'm proud to say that is the one and only time I've ever been physically thrown out of a party.

—Syracuse University

Beer Scooter

After a night on the piss, the ability to walk home 5–6 miles without noticing the distance—an almost mythical form of transportation. Also known as **Two Feet & a Heartbeat** and **Hoofing It.**

I must have ridden the beer scooter home last night.

Bent Me Over

An unpleasant result or painful conclusion to an event. Also know as **Boned** and **Reamed.**

That physics final bent me over. I should have studied.

Big Girl

No not a fat girl, but one who takes off her own pants—not waiting for the guy.

Bijiggety

To be all crazy over a guy.

Bobo

When something is f*cked up and doesn't work properly.

Money, your bike with the flat tire is so bobo.

Boffing

To have sexual relations.

Boo

A term of endearment for a boyfriend or girlfriend.

Jen's my boo.

Boof

To steal. Often used when discussing lighters.

He just left without chipping in on the pizza, AND he boofed my lighter.

[Advice: Don't want your stuff boofed? Simple solution: lock your freakin' door. Most people don't since it's a pain to always remember to lock it. But it's more of pain to listen to CDs without a stereo.]

Boojie

Short for Bourgeois. Someone who is shallow and pretentious.

Boonies

Far out of the way, away from campus and/or civilization. Usually where you have to park your car in the student lot or the location of the off campus party you had to walk to.

> **"Are We There Yet?"**
> Here's the spectrum in order of distance to pain-in-the-ass ratio:
>
> **Boonies** = a healthy walk
>
> **Guam** = past the boonies
>
> **Bum F' Nowhere (BFN)** = across a major road
>
> **Bum F' Kentucky (BFK)** = new zip code
>
> **Butt F' Egypt (BFE)** = no cell service
>
> **East Bum F' (EBF)** = middle of nowhere, usually where your car breaks down on your first roadtrip with someone's parents' car.

Booze Snooze

A nap taken early in the afternoon to prepare for the night's party, after you've already been drinking. Also known as **Party Nap**.

Boss

A girlfriend or boyfriend. Refers to their power and control over scarce resources, like sex.

Bowhead

A sorority girl who wears those big-ass bows on the back of her head to class, to the pool, and even while jogging in those nylon shorts with sorority letters on her butt.

Breaking the Seal

Going pee pee for the first time during the night. Once the seal is broken, restroom trips become much more frequent. Also known as **FFP** (Fatal First Pee). Usually, followed by an **ISP** (Inevitable Second Piss).

Break out

The act of leaving a party without telling anyone. People at the party only notice a few minutes later—depending on your popularity.

Let's break out. This party has too much sausage.

Bubble Letters

A sickly sweet font face used only by sorority girls with paint pens to adorn coolers, mugs, and little sippy water bottles.

Budget

An adjective used to describe things that are overrated, trashy, fake, or just really cheap. Can be used to refer to people, inanimate objects, towns, parties, and lunchmeat. Also known as **Sketchy, Boot-legged, Discount, Ghetto,** or **Bush League.**

The band last night was like a budget Beastie Boys.

Buffalo Club

A ritual often practiced by freshmen that requires drinking with one's opposite hand. If caught drinking otherwise, the guilty party is forced to finish their drink. Also known as **Bullmoose Club** or **Camel Club** (in Louisiana).

Bye Felicia

If a tool from down the hall keeps coming in your room talking about shiznit, this phrase is used to shoo them away. The term comes from the movie "Friday."

C

Camel Toe

When a girl's privates hang out on both sides of her panties, swimsuit, or overly tight pants. The female version of **Hanging Brains**.

Cankles

When one's calves and ankles meld together into one indistinguishable form.

Cash Cow

An ATM.

[Advice: Despite taking Spanish in high school, do not attempt to work a Cash Cow on Spanish mode for the heck of it. People do it every semester and get their cards eaten.]

Centurion

A drinking competition that consists of consuming one shot of beer every minute for 100 minutes. You may not leave your chair for any reason, nor expel any bodily fluids. Also known as **Century Club**.

CFM

Short for Come F*ck Me. An adjective for women's clothing or shoes that get guys all worked up.

Dude, didn't you see that hottie wearing those black CFM boots to class?

Chachi

A cheesy male who thinks he's got game.

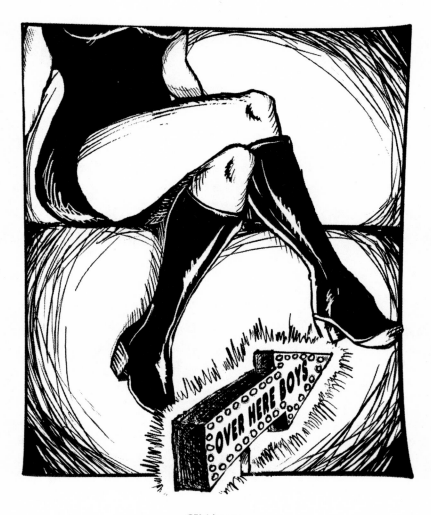

CFM boots

Chat Up

To speak to someone with the goal of getting them in bed.

Chew 'n Screw

When you eat at a restaurant or diner and run out on the bill. Also known as **Dine 'n Dash.**

Cleat Chaser

Girls (or guys) that want to get with athletes.

Clock in

Visit a boyfriend/girlfriend out of obligation and fear. Also known as **Punch the clock.**

I'd love to drink and throw stuff off the roof with you guys, but I have to clock in with the boss or she'll cut me off.

Cock Block

When one guy interferes with another guy's efforts to score. Also known as **CB,** for short.

Commando

Not wearing any underwear. Also known as **Free Ballin'** (men only).

I haven't done laundry in so long, I have to go commando today.

[Advice: Going commando isn't always a choice. Sometimes poor laundry planning makes it necessary to do without drawers. So buy plenty of undies and keep a spare pair at the bottom of the drawer.]

Convo

Short for conversation. Not really necessary, unless you are too busy to use whole words.

Crack the Spine

Opening a book for the first time. Often takes place on the night before finals.

Crotch Rot

Any number of fungi that cause extreme itchiness and discomfort in the under-carriage area. Also known as **Cratch** (crack+itch) and **Critch** (crotch+itch).

Crunchy

Describing hippie-like, outdoorsy, free spirit, tree-hugging, granola-eating, no-pit-shaving, drum-circle-dancing behavior.

D

Daisy Chain

The linkages between people via hook ups.

I don't know, Barry, it's a pretty short daisy chain between you and your roommate.

Daisy Dukes

Short-shorts made from cut-off jeans. Usually a good thing. But not always.

REAL COLLEGE MEMORY:
"Roommate's Shorts Ain't Right"

At the beginning of our senior year, my roommate Chug and I were given the opportunity to rent a nearby house. We knew the girls that were leaving, and they put in a good word with their landlord for us. It was a great deal; not only could we move into a larger, cleaner place, but the rent was about $100 per month cheaper than what we were paying. Naturally, we agreed to take it.

The house had two bedrooms and a den. We decided to reduce our expenses further by taking in another roommate. Chug knew a guy named Matty who was eager to ditch his current accommodations. If we had known how annoying Matty really was, we would have paid the extra few bucks and not brought him in as a roommate.

We suspected that Matty was not quite normal when he began to put up posters in his room. He decorated his room in the same way that a junior high girl would decorate her locker. There were posters of couples necking on top of cars and male models (probably non-threatening ones named Corey). Matty wasn't gay, but just very vain and insecure about his looks.

This was only the beginning of Matty's disturbing behavior. The guy constantly paraded around in a pair of cut-off shorts that can best be described as Daisy Dukes (complete with the holes in the ass and crotch). Matty delighted in going "Hey guys!" and then flashing us his boys when we turned around. The first time it was funny, but we soon got tired of Matty showing us his scrote.

Luckily, Matty was going out of town for the summer. I had just graduated but was sticking around for a month. The moment Matty left, Chug took over Matty's room and began tearing all of the posters off the wall and tossing all his personal papers into the closet. He even disconnected Matty's computer and began using it as a doorstop. Of course, I just laughed my ass off.

I wasn't going to be around when he returned. Besides, Chug had made plans to evict Matty promptly upon his return. Goodbye, you freak.

—University of Alberta

Dank

Something that's extremely good.

There was a dank kegger on Frat Row.

DD

Short for Designated Driver. Possibly the most prestigious title to hold for the evening. Maybe second only to Dr. Underpants.

Dead Week

The week before finals when everything is quiet and sucky.

Deboed

Pronounced DEE-BO-ed. To steal something from someone. From the movie "Friday." Also known as **Gank**.

I just deboed the hell out of your seat.

Deja Booty

1. A situation in which an individual reunites with a former fling in a seemingly random—and often ironic—twist of fate.
2. A rare instance when one hooks up with a seemingly new person only to realize that they had hooked up in the past but forgot.

Desperado

A guy/girl who roams the party looking for a last minute hook-up out of desperation.

Dick Tricks

A repertoire of maneuvers that involve a series of poses a guy can do with his exposed unit. Often used to trick people into looking at it. Motivation is inexplicable.

[Advice: Don't look down if someone wants to show you any of these: Dinner Roll, Fruit Salad, Baby Cardinal, a Pet Monkey, or the dreaded Tea Bag.]

Dirty

Used to describe an individual who has been around the block a few times. Might imply STDs or simply poor hygiene.

Watch out. She looks innocent, but she's dirty.

DOA

Short for Drunk On Arrival. Describes getting drunk before going to a party, club or class.

This party might be good, but I think we should be DOA just to be safe.

Doorknob

A game played when somebody farts. The person breaking wind must yell "safety" before the others yell "doorknob," or they get to pound the crap out of him until he grabs a doorknob. (Notice we said "him." Women don't often indulge in this.)

Double-Fisting

The art of holding and consuming two drinks at once in order to get drunk more efficiently and reduce trips to the fridge or bar.

Drop Trou

To take off one's pants.

DTR

Short for Determine the Relationship. An inevitable, yet painful, discussion that must take place in any relationship lasting longer than two weeks.

Barry and I had a DTR last night. I think we're now exclusive.

DUI

Short for Dialing Under the Influence. Includes prank calling, booty calls, and other ill-advised telecommunications. Also known as **Drunk Dialing**.

[Advice: This is usually harmless unless you are making long distance calls or falling asleep while talking on your cell. Then you'll have a surprise when you open your next bill.]

E

ELF

Short for Every Lady's Friend. That guy with a lot of hot girl friends but no chance to hook up with them.

[Advice: What an ELF might lack in immediate hook up chances, he can make up for in the long run. Since he's often in the right place at the right time, an ELF might have some action fall into his lap.]

Exit Strategy

The plan to get out of a relationship—usually developed after the second date. See entry for **Mass Dumpings**.

F

F-Bomb

Euphemism for the "F" word. And we ain't talkin' fromage.

Barry went ape shit and dropped the F-bomb in front of his parents by mistake.

[Advice: Even the most goody-two-shoes can pick up some bad language habits in the hallowed dorm halls. But be careful to turn it off when you head back home for the holidays.]

Federal

Something that's extremely good.

FFF

1. Short for Forced Family Fun. Activities that involve the whole family. Prevalent over breaks and involve crowding into mini-vans.
2. Short for Feed, F*ck, Finance. When a male who wants to be more than a friend starts asking bug-a-boo questions, then you ask him the 3-F question, "Do you FFF me, Barry? Then step off."

Fifteen-Minute Rule

If a professor is over 15 minutes late, the class may leave and not expect any repercussions. If a TA teaches the class, the time is shortened considerably.

First-year

The politically correct term for a freshman. Do not hang with people who insist on using this term.

Barry thought the she was a first-year, but she's actually a sophomore in high school.

Fix Stuff

To break stuff. An alcohol or sexual-frustration fueled rage common in males at 2:00 am—often involving bottle breaking and chest pounding. Usually accompanied by loud metal music.

Flip a bitch

To make a sharp left or a U-turn.

Flip 'n F*ck

A small futon, which is a small uncomfortable seat that folds out into a small uncomfortable mattress. Despite the name, rarely is it employed in bumpin' uglies due to its small uncomfortable-ness.

Float a Keg

To finish all the beer, thus making the keg float in its icy bath. Also known as **Kill a Keg** or **Kick a Keg.**

FNGs

Short for F*cking New Guys. New initiates to any club, fraternity, or team.

Foley Points

Props and respect for being a badass. Inspired by the famous pro wrestler Mick Foley.

Fix Stuff

REAL COLLEGE MEMORY:
"Fat Farm's Foley Points"

The Fat Farm is a bunch of over 300-pound boys from Abraham Baldwin Agricultural College. The Farm has a long tradition of ritual violence in the form of professional wrestling. Our league, the FFWA (Fat Farm Wrestling Association), differed from real pro wrestling in one critical way: it's real. At any moment we have World, Intercontinental, Tag Team, Cruiserweight, and Hardcore Champions, and a cinematic position of "President," who is able to set the matches.

One Pay Per View night, I had upset our current President, Silky, so he ordered me to fight in a Hardcore Gauntlet Match. The idea of such a match is that I would take each Farmer on, one-on-one, right after the other. Of course, it didn't go that way. Silky conspired with the rest of the Farmers, and when the bell rang, they all jumped at me with chairs, bats, empty kegs, ladders, spare tires, and any conceivable hardcore weapon. I fought them back bravely for all of 30 seconds before they mobbed me to the ground.

They proceeded to beat me for about 15 minutes, and for the most part it didn't hurt too much. Tank, a smaller but strong Farmer, was inflicting most of the punishment to me, driving a steel chair into my leg like a spear, while most of the others just ineffectively beat on my protective layer of fat and muscle.

I knew I was in trouble when Big Dog set up the ladder beside me. Then, like King Kong, the 350-pounder climbed to the top. In desperation, I considered rolling out of the way, but I knew there was no avoiding the inevitable; the Farmers would just beat me until this coup de grace was delivered. So I lay there and drew in a deep breath in an effort to cushion the impact.

Like a great, lardy bird of prey, Big Dog dive-bombed from the top of the 10-foot ladder and gracefully fell through the air in a sky-eclipsing belly flop. It seemed like an hour passed as he rushed down on me and my mind panicked through many possible solutions to this very grave problem I was facing.

I heard later, from those in attendance, that the collision was breathtakingly beautiful, akin to the Shuemaker-Levy comet striking the surface of Jupiter. There was surprisingly little pain, for my part, just a series of popping noises and the strange feeling of my sternum striking my backbone. I lay there, deaf and dumb, coughing up fluids and aching. Then, after a half-hour, I slowly rose to my feet to the awe of the wrestlers and hangers-on. A cheer erupted as I began to fight in my next match of the evening.

I lost that match, but still acquired quite a bit of Foley points for having the balls to fight once again.

—Abraham Baldwin Agricultural College

Food condition

The dramatic ups and downs that come from not eating all day then gorging yourself—ranges from cranky to hyper to insane.

FOS

Short for Full of Shit.

404

Describes someone who is clueless.

She was all 404 when it came to dating.

Freshmen 15

The legendary weight-gain experienced after one's first year in school.

Frisbee

Any uneaten pizza left on the floor of a dorm room.

FUBU

Short for F*ck Buddy. A FUBU understands that there is no relationship beyond sex.

I have to meet up with my FUBU later for a little private time.

FUPA

Short for Fat Upper Pelvic Area. Also known as the **Roll** and after a few pounds the **Buddha**.

G

GDI

Short for God Damn Independents. How Greeks often refer to non-Greeks.

What's up with those GDIs drinking our beer and hitting on our women? Let's go act tough.

Get a Room

An expression used when two people are displaying their mutual affection publicly and it would benefit everyone's digestive tracts if they would go into a private area before doing the hippity-dippity out in the open. Often yelled across the bar to said couple.

Get the Heisman

To get one's advances rejected. Comes from the stiff-arm pose of the Heisman Trophy. Also known as **Broke Off** and **Shaq'ed**.

[Advice: No one likes to get the Heisman. If you are the giver of one, be polite to your advancer. But, if he's being an aggressive jag-off, let him have it.]

Go dark

When a person is unreachable despite their having a cell phone, pager, etc.

Golf Party

A party in which participants form teams and go from room to room taking various shots of alcohol. Similar to **Around the World.**

Got five on it

A rule that allows an individual to leave his/her seat in a room and return within five minutes and still retain rights to sit there.

Get the Heisman

Granola

Something or someone who is crunchy/outdoorsy/hippyish.

Gravy

Describes something that's easy or extra good.

Greek Freak

A new pledge who is super absorbed in sorority/fraternity goings-on. Often sports a fraternity credit card, sweatshirt, license plate, tattoos, and even book covers.

Gump

A person who somehow always seems to be in the right place at the right time. These people always have the best stories, but they can never be verified.

H

Hallcest

The dangerous act of getting with someone on your hall.

[Advice: Much like in MTV's "Real World," hallcest will lead to drama, yelling, and great viewing for everyone else. Hallcest is not a recommended practice.]

Handle

A 1.5-liter bottle of hard liquor. Named after the handle often crafted into the bottle. Also known as **Home Wrecker.**

Hang Brains

When a guy's testicles can be seen poking out of the legs of his shorts or swim trunks. The male version of the **Camel Toe.** Also known as **Showin' Scrote** and **Letting the Mouse out of the House**.

Hell Week

Greek term for a most grueling week before initiation when pledgeship increases in intensity. Sleep and grades take backseats to rituals involving paddles, the Greek alphabet, and eating the dreaded olive out of your pledge brother's butt.

Hitting the Snooze Bar

To continue to hook up with someone even though you should really break up. Prolonging the inevitable.

HMB

Short for High Maintenance Boys. Guys who take an unusually long time to get ready to go out. Also known as **Pretty Boys**.

Are the HMB's here or are they still primping?

Hang Brains

Hoggin'

The practice of hooking up with large, hefty individuals.

Hook Up

A romantic or sexual encounter of any varying degrees of intimacy.

[Advice: This term can mean something very different to different people. Rumors can spread when someone misinterprets and assumes it means the "deed" rather than a peck.]

Hoss

Very masculine and manly. Often refers to women who exhibit man-like characteristics or play on the varsity softball team.

Hotboxing

1. Smoking lots of pot in a small, contained area, such as a car or single dorm room, making the air so smoky that you are taking a hit every time you breathe. Also known as **Fishbowling, Greenhousing,** or **Clambaking**.
2. A sorority term referring to a type of rush infraction in which too many girls talk to a potential new member at one time.

Hour of Power

Drinking 60 shots of beer in 60 minutes. Ironically the Hour of Power often zaps your energy. Also known as **Power Hour**.

Huey

An individual who tries way too hard to impress their teacher in class. Also known as a **Kiss Ass** and **Brown Noser**.

Hunch Punch

A potent concoction prepared with care by the party hosts. Usually includes grain alcohol, powdered punch, diced fruit, and a healthy dose of water from a garden hose. It's mixed in a trashcan or drinking trough—lovingly stirred with a broken Wiffle® ball bat or broom handle. Also known as **Jungle Juice**.

[Advice: Be careful of this stuff. Might include dangerous additives or just gross ones. Make sure you trust the maker—or you might meet your maker.]

Hurt Locker

A place of extreme discomfort.

After I mooned those townies, they caught me and put my ass in the hurt locker.

I

IPS

Instant Princess Syndrome. This phenomenon affects females who get huge egos from the excess attention caused by being in an environment with an overabundance of sausage. Also known as **GAS** (Guy Attention Syndrome).

You know Sandy with the lazy eye: she got a bad case of IPS.

Invisible

To be drunk.

"Let's Get Pissed!"
Anyone (of legal drinking age) can drink and get drunk, but it takes talent to use silly names to describe it. Drink responsibly, but talk about it with wild abandon.

12 oz. power curls, Abbreviated, Anchored, Anesthetized, Arrested, Barley basted, Battered, Bent, Bitched, Black and Tanned, Bladdered, Blasted, Blazed, Blitzed, Blocked, Bolloxed (Irish), Bombed, Bowled over, Buggered, Bullet Proof, Canned, Captured, Chemically inconvenienced, Chiseled, Clarked, Clobbered, Clocked, Cockailed, Cocked, Corked, Cranked, Crapped out, Crazy ass-ed, Crocked, Crusted, Curled, Dead to the World, Deflated, Demolished, Destroyed, Dilled, Disinfected, Done, Drafted, Drinky, stinky, Drowned, Drowning, Drunker than Cooter Brown, Dusted, Erased, Encrypted, Etherized, Excused, Faced, Faded, Fer Shnickered, Fermented, Fertilized, Flagged, Flattened, Floored, Flushed, Four sheets to the wind, Fricasseed, Fried, Frosted, FUBAR, Full of Dutch courage, Gassed, Getting stupid, Going out to forget our names, Gone, Hammered, Hoganed (as in Hulk Hogan), Hosed, Housed, In rare form, In the Bag, Invincible, Jacked, Juiced, Kablitzed, Lagered, Lambasted, Legless, Looped, Loopy, Lost in the sauce, Lubricated, Maggoted, Marinated, Mashed, Messed, Mothered, Mutilated, Nastified, Neutered (Australian), Numbed, Obliterated, Out of commission, Out of your gourd, Overserved, Paddled, Peppered, Pickled, Pirate-eyed, Pixilated, Polexed (Irish), Pruned, Rat faced, Red-eyed, Refunded, Rotten,

Rounded, Rum dumb, Salted, Shellacked, Shelled, Slaughtered, Sledged, Slizzard, Smashed, Soaked, Sozzled, Spanked, Stonkered, Stupified, Tanked, Tequilafied, Thumped, To' up from the Flo' up, Toasted, Unglued, Waxed, Wilted, Zonked, Zooted

J

Jailbait

A hot high school girl. Also known as a **Felony** or **JV** (Junior Varsity).

[Advice: Don't assume because you meet someone on campus that they are of age. You'd be surprised how many visiting siblings get broken off some.]

Jamaican Bobsled Team

A group of stoners who dress in Rastafarian gear.

JBF Hair

Short for Just Been F*cked Hair. It refers to the messed up hair that is usually experienced on the walk of shame or after waking up from a fun night out partying.

[Advice: JBF hair is just one more reason to always have a baseball cap within reach. You'll also find this helpful during finals when showering is too time consuming.]

Jersey Chaser

A lady who only wants to get with football/basketball players.

Justice

Devine karma that good things happen to good people and jerks usually get their just desserts.

When that preachy guy from Team Jesus got caught cheating, it was pure justice.

Jamaican Bobsled Team

REAL COLLEGE MEMORY:
"Justice for an Underage Drinker"

The date was 9/9/99. I should have known this ominous date could only spell trouble. It was the third week of fraternity rush, and I had limited my choices to two. I began the night at the first frat, where we played a variety of drinking games with hard alcohol, which I don't do too well with. I spent about two hours at this place, leaving there around 10 p.m.

At that point I left with my friend "Ja-Ja," named after Jar-Jar Binks for being so damn annoying. We had to go a mere one block down and two blocks over to get to the other frat we were rushing. But Ja-Ja and I were not very coherent, and we ended up going two blocks over and one block down. Not good. We had absolutely no clue where we were. Then the cops came by. I spotted them first and alertly yelled "PIGS" at the top of my lungs, then began to skip away—not run, not walk, not trot mildly, SKIP.

I skipped up the front walkway of a private residence, opened their front door and went in. Inside, I saw the man and woman who lived there and promptly turned around. When I got back to the front door, Officer Hill met me there. Officer Hill turned out to be a relatively nice man. He issued me a portable Breathalyzer test, which I didn't do so well on. He then issued me two citations, one for underage drinking, and another for public drunkenness, noting on each of them that I called the police "pigs." Great.

They put me in handcuffs and gave me a ride back to my dorm. I found out the combined total of my fines was going to be $325, a hefty fee, as I'm sure any fellow student can appreciate. But don't fear my story takes a turn for the better. Two days later, I was sitting at dinner with a friend, a dinner that I only went to because they were having chicken wings. When a man started spouting about a game show he was hosting at our student union building that night, called "DA$H FOR DOLLAR$," my friend looked up from his spaghetti and meatballs and joked, "You should go, maybe you can pay off your fines." I said, "What the hell, things can't get any worse."

The game worked like this: Three rounds, four contestants each round. Everyone in the crowd put their name in the box, and contestants were drawn at random. First round went by, nada. It was the baby round; games included chugging OJ from a baby bottle. Second round went by, nada. Hawaiian round—games like limbo. I guarantee I wouldn't have won that one; tall white guys don't do well in limbo. Third round went by, nada. But wait, not nada. The fourth guy in the round wasn't there. So they pulled another name, and wouldn't ya know it, they pulled mine.

My round was a sports round—money in the bank. First game was ring toss; I went first and hit 5/10, so I was in. Next game was mini-free throws, with one of those Fisher-Price basketball nets. Now as I said before, I'm tall, and lanky, so my long arms made it easy, and I moved on. Final game was mini-golf putting with a 2-foot putter into a circle a foot wide 5 feet away. I'm money at mini-golf, and I made my first shot, stunning the host. The other guy missed, so I won my heat, gaining $25, and the chance to square off against the other round winners for a chance at the grand prize. Same rules, two elimination games.

First game was walking back and forth with 20 pennies stacked up on a wooden spoon, first to drop theirs, loses. I somehow held off the one guy, despite my hand shaking like a leaf. That left me and some other guy for all the marbles.

They brought out two paper plates with whipped cream on them. Somewhere in our plates was a wrapped piece of Bubble Yum bubble gum. We had to find the gum with our face, unwrap it, blow a bubble the size of a half-dollar, and hold it for 5 seconds. Easier said than done, however. What they didn't tell us was that the whipped cream was shortening, and it's physically impossible to blow a bubble until you chew it all out. The other guy found his gum right away. I struggled to find mine, and when I finally did, I couldn't unwrap it. So I threw it in my mouth with the wrapper on. I somehow got mine to bubble after about a minute, and won.

The grand prize was thirty seconds in a money cube (you know the things, they blow dollar bills all around and you keep what you grab). In the cube there was a total of $500: one $100 and a bunch of smaller bills. They gave me a pouch into which I could stuff the money. I also opened up my tucked-in baseball jersey half way thinking that some might fly in (and not out). So I went in. And went at it.

Of course everyone wanted to know if I got the $100, so the host went through the chamber and didn't see it. I went through my pile, and I didn't see it, either. So where was it? I looked in my shirt, and it was the only bill that flew in there. Swear to God. It was like something out of a TV show. I pulled it out triumphantly to a huge ovation from the crowd.

I wound up coming out with $235 plus the $25 from before, a total of $260. It didn't totally pay off my fines, but it made for a hell of a two-day turnaround and proof that there is justice out there.

—Penn State University

K

Kelly Capwell Effect

A really hot girl who ends up having every guy she meets fall in love with her. Refers to a character from the old soap "Santa Barbara."

Kelvin Club

The rare feat of having a GPA that equals absolute zero.

Kids

One's testicles. Also known as **The Boys** or **Scrote**.

That line drive came dangerously close to connecting with my kids.

REAL COLLEGE MEMORY:
"Hanging from the Kids"

Way back in the fall of 1994, I had the pleasure of sharing a dorm room with a certain half-Spanish boy by the name of Timoteo, or Tight Pants Tim, as his friends know him. Quite a debonair young fellow, nothing funny ever really happened to him. He never tripped and fell in the middle of campus with all the football players watching, he never went ass over teacups off his 10-speed bike while trying to get to class on time, and he never got laughed at because he knocked himself out with a textbook...no, that stuff was left for me to do. Timoteo was just too suave. That is, until new mattress day.

I shared a dorm room with Timoteo and another guy in one of the better dormitories on campus. It was your typical college dorm room: complete with black-light Cypress Hill posters on the wall, brand new textbooks still in their shrink-wrap strewn about, and the ever present aroma of dirty feet, ramen noodles, and a hint of bong water. There was a single bed on one side of the room and a bunk bed, which Timoteo and I used, on the other side. For anyone who knows anything about dorm room bunk beds, they know that craftsmanship leaves much to be desired, rivaling only prison bunks in their shoddiness. Underneath these old, worn out mattresses were hundreds of exposed springs and hooks, kind of a "built-in" box spring, with rusted metal jutting out in every direction.

One fine autumn day, the school decided to give our dorm new mattresses for all of these horrible beds—sticking to their plan of replacing dormitory bedware every 40 years or so! It was our job as dorm residents to throw the old mattresses on the floor so the maintenance staff could easily switch them out. As it was still early in the day, Timoteo was in his boxer shorts watching *Little House On The Prairie*, just lounging on the top bunk. Our good friend Jason had just stopped by as well, hoping we'd be ready to go out and get something to eat. And that's when it happened. That's when I witnessed the funniest thing I have ever seen in my entire life, EVER!

Reminding us that the mattresses were being replaced later that day, Jason took the mattress off the single bed and threw it into the middle of the room. I followed suit with the mattress to the bottom bunk. Then Timoteo, still lay-ing around in his underwear, threw his top bunk mattress onto the other two in the center of our little room. With all three mattresses safely on the floor, Jason and I patiently sat on them waiting for Timoteo to get down and get dressed so we could finally go eat. Seemingly in no rush at all, Timoteo just sat on the edge of the "mattress-less" top bunk with his legs hanging off of the side wearing only his boxer shorts and a smile. That smile, however, would quickly morph into a horrific grimace and piercing yelp like nothing I'd ever before heard from a human.

As the three of us talked and joked, Timoteo finally decided it was time to get down from the bunk and start his day. That's when disaster struck. As he pushed himself off the side of the top bunk's metal bed frame to leap down onto the floor, his boxer shorts became caught on one of the bed's exposed hooks!

Like a rag doll, his limp legs came crashing down into the frame of the lower bunk and his arms slammed into the frame of the upper one. All one could hear was the crash of skin to metal and the even more violent sound of a man's genitalia being crushed into his ass pipe. He was dangling there, a foot off of the ground, hanging on by the waistline of his underwear. His kids ripped violently into his rear, poor Timoteo just writhed in pain, struggling to free himself. It looked like he was wearing a g-string…backwards. All he could do was scream for help, but Jason and I were too busy laughing our asses off to even attempt a rescue. (Jason literally pissed his pants from laughing so hard.)

I eventually tried to aide him by bear-hugging his sack-less torso attempt-ing to pull him free from his crotch terror. But I couldn't muster enough strength due to my own violent laughter, not to mention my lack of content-ment with the fact that he was practically naked. Timoteo dangled there for several minutes until the weight of his fat gut and gravity finally won out.

Suddenly, his cotton underwear gave way to the immense, fraught mass, and he landed on his ass with a tremendous thud. Yowling in pain, he wad-dled to the bathroom, his swollen parts protruding from the back of his new thong undies. Looking like a sumo wrestler with the reddest ass ever, he cried out unto the heavens as he raced down the hall for help. In one fell swoop, Timoteo had gone from suave and debonair to still suave and debonair but with a great story about him getting his wiener shoved into his own ass.

—University of Florida

Killer

A term used to describe a ridiculously overheated individual. Also known as **Tiger** or **Cowboy**.

Calm down there killer, no one stole your blankie.

Kings

A drinking game played with an edited deck of cards; often encourages rhyming, revenge, and drinking a nasty cup of warm brew.

KleptoMode

What happens after you've drank too much and all you want to do is steal because you think you're slicker than grease. Often performed by **Sneaky Drunks**.

L

Lay pipe

To have sex.

Lesbian in a Bottle

The magical quality of a bottle of liquor that causes straight girls to make out with other girls. Also known as a **Two-Beer Queer.**

> **"Sex Synonyms"**
> Some people call it making love. Some people call it the hippity-dippity. We call it one of the following:
>
> **Beat it up** - "I heard you beat it up last night."
> **Merck** - "Did I see you and Barry merking last night?"
> **Smashing** - "Were you two smashing last night?"
> **Wax** - "Dude, I got waxed last night"
>
> Also known as Banging, Bashing, Beating, Boinking, Bumpin' Uglies, Hitting It, Jabbing, Knocking boots, Knocking It, Piling, Pumping, Tapping it, Womping on.

Lightweight

One who is unable to handle their alcohol. Also known as a **Two-Beer Queer.** The opposite of a **Heavyweight.**

[Advice: Be careful to use the right context with the term Two Beer Queer. It's got two different meanings.]

Liquid Encouragement

Refers to how alcohol can help you be able to talk or attempt to talk to anyone. Also known as **Liquid Courage.**

Loving Life

Having an exceedingly good time.

When Brett had to tutor the cheerleading squad, he was loving life.

LUG

Short for Lesbian Until Graduation. Label given to those "lesbians" who are just experimenting and will likely switch teams (back to straight) once they graduate.

Lung Candy

Cigarettes. Also known as **Cancer Sticks, Smokey Treats,** or **Grit** (Southern).

[Advice: Smoking is a personal decision. But be warned, many people who try to quit later in life started smoking in college. It's very easy to start on most campuses, so just make sure it is a habit you want to have for years to come. And no, your parents didn't pay us to say this.]

M

Mangina

A **Dick Trick** that involves, er, maybe you should just rent "Silence of the Lambs" to see for yourself. Also known as the **Hideaway**.

Marinate

The art of doing absolutely nothing. Also known as **Hangin'** or **Chillin'**.

Mass Dumpings

Traditional times throughout the year, when students execute simultaneous dumpings of significant others. The opposite is the **No-Breakup Zone**: the period of time in between Christmas and Spring Break when it is usually most difficult to meet and date new people due to the Holidays.

> **"It's Not You, It's Your Personality"**
> Everyone on campus is on the same cycle. And when it comes to relationships, sometimes you need to make a timely break to prevent future problems or to take advantage of new opportunities. Here are some common mass dumpings:
>
> **Turkey Dump** — before Thanksgiving break and more importantly before holiday gift giving.
>
> **Spring-cleaning** — before spring break, one must have freedom for the week.
>
> **Hat Toss** — a week or two after graduation to clear the dating slate for the summer.
>
> Take note: after each dumping there are more singles on the market—good for anyone trolling for a mate.

Mattress

A guy/girl who has slept with multiple members of a Greek organization or team. Also known as **Frattress** and **Fraturniture.**

Here comes the Mattress, watch out for VD!

McGrubbies

Food.

Dude, I'm starving. Let's go snag some McGrubbies.

Meathead

A guy of low intelligence and a thick neck. Often chosen to be your lab partner.

Ménage-A-Deux

What you must first achieve before you can hope to get a ménage-a-trois.

Mexican Shower

The practice of washing just your face and pits in the sink. While racist, the term is used by students of all ethnicities. Don't confuse it with a **Whores' Bath** in which one just washes their genitals.

[Advice: If you don't mind the smell, baby wipes can be good substitutes for showers during road trips or extended periods of laziness.]

MILF

Abbreviation for Mother I'd Love to F*ck. There is no equivalent for dads due to lack of need for such a term. Also known as a **Cougar**.

Money Tree

An ATM.

Mr./Ms. Diversity

Someone who serially hooks up with individuals of a different race/ethnicity than their own. Also known as an **EOH** (Equal Opportunity Ho/Hookup).

Mr. T Starter Kit

Excessive gold jewelry worn around the neck (usually by a trashy male).

Dude, where did you get that Mr. T Starter kit? No one wears gold chains any more.

M.R.S. Degree

Refers to a marriage license. For some girls it is the sole purpose of going to college or joining a certain sorority. Of course, they're usually looking for a "suitable" husband from a wealthy family to graduate with honors and earn this degree.

Mule

An individual, often male, who doesn't give a shit about his dignity or safety and will accept any bet or challenge regardless of better judgment.

I can't believe Barry ate thirty eggs for $2. What a mule.

REAL COLLEGE MEMORY:
"The Mule and the Spittoon"

Here's a story about one of the biggest mules ever to come out of Hartford. His name was Grant. Grant had inherited a ton of money in his teens when both his parents died. He didn't go to school. In fact he didn't do much of anything other than sit around drinking, doing drugs, and hanging with us students.

In Hartford, back in the day, there was a bar called the Russian Lady. It was over by the Civic Center and was a popular hangout before and after Whalers games. And in the Russian Lady, in the corner, there was a spittoon. This is the story of why they got rid of it.

I was there one night, with Louie and Grant. And Grant noticed the spittoon, brimming with a noxious and possibly toxic mixture of tobacco juice from any number of contributors over the course of the past week. Grant called the bartender over. "Hey man," he said, "If I drink the contents of that spittoon, you have to let me drink free for the night." The bartender of course looked at Grant like he had casually admitted to having a cellar full of corpses. (Which, come to think of it, is not out of the realm of possibility.) Then he said, "Yeah, whatever," just humoring Grant. Or so he thought.

So Grant walked over to the corner and picked up the spittoon and raised it to his lips, the contents sloshing over the side and running down his fingers. Meanwhile, the bar had grown silent as several dozen people stood transfixed by the unfolding horror.

Grant touched his lips to the edge, a strand of viscous gunk dripping down his chin. From somewhere there was the sound of a muffled female scream. He took a sip. People freaked out. "Dude!" the bartender yelled, "Okay! Okay! You proved your point! Stop it!"

Grant pauses for a second, takes a breath, and then proceeds to: CHUG THE ENTIRE CONTENTS OF THE SPITTOON. People screamed.

Honest to god, they all screamed. From the edge of the bar a preppy Trinity College-looking chick puked all over the bar. Two people ran outside to be sick in the snow.

Grant drained the last of the contents and put the spittoon on the bar. Long streams of saliva ran down his chest. The bartender was white as a sheet. "Good God, you asshole. I gave in! Why did you do that?" the bartender asked.

"Hey," Grant stated simply, "I was on a roll."

—Assumption College

N

Nap Zap

That sudden jerk that happens when you are dozing off. A dead giveaway when it happens in class—or on a date.

Navy Seal

When you have to pull a mission impossible because your friend is hooking up with the cute girl, but they brought the ugly friend. So you have to take one for the team. Also known as **Jump On The Grenade.**

NCL

Short for Non-Committal Lip. When you can make out with someone with no strings attached.

It's ok; I have NCL for the weekend.

[Advice: While this sounds great, it is often an illusion. There are often many strings attached.]

> **"The Dorkiness Scale"**
> Go from Zero to Tool Box in 30 Seconds
>
> Here are some common terms for annoying individuals. Enjoy, dorks.
>
> **Zero** — A person with nothing to offer. Also known as a **Null Set.**
>
> **Packing Peanut** — An unwanted person who's always hanging all over you.
>
> **Hanging Chad** — One that follows you around a lot. Also known as a **Chafe.**
>
> **Beggar** — A nerdier, more annoying version.
>
> **Stain** — A person that is a pain in the ass.
>
> **Dart** — So annoying that you feel the urge to throw a dart at their face.
>
> **Tool** — A socially inept individual. Similar to a nerd, but not as smart.
>
> **Wedge** — The simplest of all tools. Even more insulting
>
> **Tool Box** — A tool with fewer redeeming characteristics like smarts or a car.

Newman

Your friend's friend that you can't stand. Taken from "Seinfeld."

O

Odd or Even

A stupid drinking game that involves guessing if the next card is, you guessed it, odd or even. Usually played at the end of the night when thinking is too difficult.

Off the Chain

Describes a person or party that is excessively wild. Also known as **Off the Hook**.

After you left the party, a bus of wrestling midgets showed up. It was off the chain.

Old Shoe

A former boyfriend/girlfriend who can be counted on for a casual hook up in a pinch.

[Advice: Breaking up is hard to do. And getting back together can be easy. But be forewarned, it is much harder to break up again after a relapse with an Old Shoe.]

OOC

Short for Out of Control.

Osmosis

Refers to a method of study employed by crammers who fall asleep with their heads on their books. Not very reliable.

I didn't study yesterday, but I was learning by osmosis last night.

Osmosis

P

Pack Up

Shut up or leave.

How you be chatting up MY man? Bitch, pack up!

Panty Dropper

A girl in general, or more specifically a slutty girl who'll sleep with anyone. Be careful how you use it as some may find it offensive—some people are so sensitive.

Parent-proof

Prepare a room for a visit from the parental units. Usually includes hiding: alcohol, birth control, controlled substances, poor test grades, and dirty dishes.

REAL COLLEGE MEMORY:
"Parent-proofing the Whores"

I think I still have the piece of paper, folded in quarters, almost tearing along each crease. On this piece of intricately flowered parchment, one of our suitemates had inscribed "THE GIRLS OF SUITE 207 ANSWER TO THE FOLLOWING." What followed was a list of obscenities, euphemisms, and everyday trucker vernacular that encompassed any term ever used to describe a whore. Eventually, the list had evolved from a harmless joke to a tableau that would make Larry Flynt blush. I'm ashamed to say that the only recollection I have of the Oxford English Dictionary being utilized by my friends is to find more synonyms for "prostitute." Having run out of actual terms, we'd even begun to string together insults; wench + Jezebel became "Wedgebel."

One weekend, my roommate's parents were coming for a visit. So like characters in a Prohibition-era movie, we had to quickly convert the speakeasy to a respectable establishment before the Feds (in this case, her parents) moved in.

Cigarette butts, ashtrays, etc. moved out. Liquor bottles were relocated from their prominent position on the dresser to the bottom of my laundry basket. Any potentially offensive magazine article or incriminating photo—removed. It must have been me doing the final parent-proofing sweep.

Meg was good at the preliminary stuff, but only someone raised in a strict Irish Catholic family could sniff out the seemingly inoffensive and explain as to how it could be construed as something evil by concerned parents. Satisfied that the room was now "parent-proofed," we went off to class.

We returned from class to find our door open. Meg's parents and brother were already there waiting. They seemed preoccupied. Her little brother was staring at something on the opposite wall, chortling silently. Confident that it couldn't be anything incriminating, Meg ignored her brother's laughter and asked her parents if they were ready to go to lunch. "Uh, sure honey," drawled her mom.

"Sure, TROLLOPES!" said her brother—pointing to the flowery scroll we'd missed in our inspection.

—Wake Forest University

Party Foul

An incident that goes against the rules of the party. For example, spilling your glass of red wine on the Dean's white carpet during an elegant mixer or mistaking the coat closet for a bathroom.

Pass the bar

To be able to walk/drive home successfully despite severe inebriation. Opposite: **To Flunk the Bar.**

[Advice: Drunk driving happens on campuses, a lot. But there are usually shuttles, cabs, or sober friends that can get you home. Use them. There's no excuse for drinking and driving. Now, back to your terms.]

PDA

Short for Public Display of Affection. Can range from kissing to dry humping on the dance floor. See also **Get a Room.**

Penalty Box

The area behind the back seat of a SUV, which usually accommodates the sixth passenger who needs a ride. Also known as **Family Dog.**

We made Barry ride home in the penalty box.

Penny the Door

Deliberately trapping someone in their room by forcefully hammering a stack of pennies between their door and the doorframe. Prevents people from getting in or out. Also known as **Pennylocking**.

REAL COLLEGE MEMORY:
"Pennylocking PJ"

Here's the back story: Jeff is a huge geek that lived across from me. He became Puking Jeff (PJ) after a bad drinking incident, and we were about to do battle. PJ had a roommate named Alex. Alex was kind of nerdy, but not near the geek PJ was. My roommate, Wally, had a deep seething dislike for Alex. Over the course of the semester, somehow or another, we ended up in a prank war with each other. Room against room.

It started out harmlessly enough. They would knock on our door at 3am and run. They would order five large pizzas to our room. And we would get back at them in all sorts of ways.

Once I even bought a gallon of milk, poured into a trash can and sat it out on our window ledge for five days. I then took it and propped it up against PJ's door at about 4am and knocked really loud. When they scrambled to open the door I was long gone, but when they opened it…splash! All over the entire room.

Well, anyway back to the story. One night, not being his normal self, Wally went out with me. We stayed out until around daylight. When we returned to our dorm room, which I should mention is on the 4th floor from the street, and 5th floor from the inside quad, we found that someone had "pennylocked" our door. I have found that a lot of people don't know what "pennylocked" is, so I will tell you. Every door has a lip that fits against the door. If you push really hard against the door, it creates a very small gap between the door and the frame. If you take roughly 6 to 10 pennies and stack them up and place them inside that gap, it makes almost any door totally impossible to open from the inside. It puts so much pressure on the door that the knob can't turn; taking off the hinges doesn't even work.

So we took out the pennies and went into our room and went across the hall and returned the favor. I then called them on the phone. When PJ answered, I told him to let us out of our room. He then said something I will never forget, nor will he. He said "Tell me, who is the Man?" I simply said "PJ, I am the man, now try to get out of your room you silly son of a bitch!"

They cried, bitched, and moaned for a long time. They begged to be let out. After a few minutes, Wally and I noticed that it got strangely quiet in their room. They weren't saying a word. What was going on? After twenty minutes, I was getting really worried. I was about to open the door, when from the stairwell came a long groaning sound. PJ's head appeared at the doorway. He was on his hands and knees. He was bleeding from both arms; his faced was badly bruised and had cuts all over it. His eyes were wide open like he had been electrocuted or something. And he was having a hard time breathing.

Wally and I picked him up to carry him to his room. I unlocked the door, and there sat Alex. He was rocking back and forth on his bed. The entire room was destroyed. The beds were over by the window, which was open. Open? It was ten degrees outside. "What the hell?" I thought. Then I noticed that a rope was tied to the bed. "OH, Shit!" I turned to Wally and he was seeing the same thing I saw. We knew what had happened.

Turns out that PJ had gotten tired of being harassed and locked in his room. So being the military minded man that he was, he bought a rope with a grappling hook on the end. He had hooked the rope to the end of his bed, and tried to climb out the window. Now, because he was in the Navy, and not the Army, he didn't know to tie knots in the rope for handholds, or to wear gloves. He also didn't know that beds move when something is tied to them and then jumps out of a window. Out of a 4th story window, he had fallen 3 1/2. Luckily some metal tipped concrete steps and a metal tube railing at the bottom broke his fall. Too embarrassed about falling, he made the climb back upstairs to get back to his room.

While carrying him to the hospital, I noticed that his entire foot was spinning as if it was not attached. Turns out it wasn't. His entire ankle was shattered. He had a severe concussion, contusions over most of his body, and severe body bruising. He was damn lucky to be alive!

That evening, I returned to my dorm room to find the door open. I walked in, and there sat PJ with who else but his Mom! He said "I hope you don't mind, we were getting something off the net and my computer isn't working."

"No problem" I said. He introduced his mom, she then started going off about how the University should be sued for letting the stairs stay wet and her son falling and hurting himself. I laughed so hard inside, you see, he was too embarrassed to tell his mom that he fallen almost 50 feet out of a window to avoid telling her something I already knew. I am the man.

—Tennessee Technological University

Permadrunk

When someone is always acting stupid, even when sober.

Pizza Bones

The uneaten crust of a pizza. Often scavenged by cheap friends like Barry down the hall.

Plead the fifth

Exercising your right to remain silent because you consumed about a fifth of liquor and cannot recall the bulk of the evening's events.

Po-Po

The police. Also known as **Bacon, Pigs,** and **Five-Oh.**

PopSodaCoke

The stupid game freshman play. Basically, you make fun of everyone who doesn't call a soft drink the same thing you do.

POS

Short for Piece of Shit. Usually refers to one's car, stereo, or part-time job.

Pre

Short for Predrinking. Often because: you are underage, alcohol is too

> ## "What Do You Call It?"
> Here's a simple guide to predicting what someone will call a soft drink:
>
> - *Pop* drinkers are mainly mid-Western and Canadian.
>
> - *Soda* drinkers are mostly from the Northeast, California, Milwaukee, and St. Louis.
>
> - *Coke* is the term for everything in the South, from the Carolinas to Texas.

expensive at this place, or it is too boring to be sober when you show up (i.e. class). Also known as **Frontloading, Pregaming, Prefunking, Warming up,** and **DOA (Drunk On Arrival).**

Wanna pre before the concert?

P's

The people who raised you, helped pay for your schooling, and initiate wild cleaning sessions before they come to visit. Also known as **Rents (Rentals)** and **Folks**.

Pulled it out of one's ass

Take a wild guess.

[Advice: Go with your gut. If you've studied for a test, but are confronted with an utterly confusing question, trust your intuition. Even if you can't recall it, the knowledge is somewhere inside that huge head of yours.]

Q

QT

Short for Quality Time. Spending time with anyone important. It can be said to the boys, "I have to spend some QT with the boss," or "I have to spend some QT with the rents and then I will hit it hard."

[Advice: Without sounding cheesy, make sure you manage your QT in college. Think about what's important in life (family, friends, academics, sports, etc.) and make an effort to spend time tending to these activities, first. Then, spend the remaining hours doing stupid stuff.]

Quarters

A drinking game involving bouncing quarters into a shot glass. Known to ruin nice tables and damage young livers.

"IT'S A FACT"
According to a 2003 survey on CollegeStories.com, here are the top drinking games played on college campuses:

Asshole	33%
Beer Pong	33%
Kings	12%
Quarters	8%
Other liver-killing games	14%

R

Rack or Re-Rack

1. Reorganizing cups in a game of beer pong—depending on house rules this is normally not required until there are only three cups remaining on one side of the table.
2. One's bed, or a term for sleeping.

After I went to my 7:30 class I had to re-rack so I could go out that night.

Rally

When you pass out or fall sleep early, but then get up and keep rocking out.

Wake up ladies, it's time to rally!

Raunching

Flirting with all the hottest guys in the place, and hooking up with as many guys as possible in one night.

Razzing

To be joking with someone.

REAL COLLEGE MEMORY:
"Cheating in the Open"

During my (second) senior year, I was taking this horrifying Probability course with my good buddy G-Dog who happens to be a math major. He is also a major wise-ass.

So the course is horrible and no matter how much we study, our grades go steadily down. We both pulled low 20's on the third test. Convinced we were both going to fail the course, we studied minimally for the final. The big day comes and the prof hands out the test. He allowed us one sheet of notes. My friend proceeds to take out the book, a few rented books, his notes, each test, each homework assignment, and a few back tests. He spreads them out and starts the test.

After a short while the professor made his way to where we were sitting and says, "Mr. Hickman, I clearly stated you can use one sheet of notes. What are you doing?" G-Dog looks at him, pauses and says the best thing I have ever heard:

"Well Professor, I think its fairly obvious, to even the most simple minded individual, that I am cheating. A lot. Next question?"

The professor was at a loss for words. So G-Dog goes, "Oh I'm just razzin' ya." He then puts the stuff away and finishes the test early. He didn't even attempt half of those problems he later told me. He gets up, hands in his test, packs up, and goes home since it was his last for the semester. He failed. I pulled a 'D' for 'Done'.

—Polytechnic University

Riding bitch

Sitting in the middle of the car's backseat. The worst position for road trips unless you are between two hotties.

[Advice: If you know a road trip will require a few pit stops, volunteer to ride bitch early on—before things get claustrophobic and stinky.]

Rip a new one

To be yelled at with severity.

When the RA caught us with the goat, he ripped us a new one.

Ripped

Muscular and fit. Also known as **Cock Diesel**.

Rough

Ugly.

That guy's face is a little rough.

"What to Call an Ugly Person"

These terms all refer to a person of the opposite sex who looks good from far away but gets progressively worse as you get closer:

- Monet
- Transformer
- DDF (Distance Distortion Factor)
- Fifty-Yard Fake

These are people with good bods but nothing redeeming from the neck up:

- B.O.B.F.O.C. (Body off Baywatch, Face off Crime Watch)
- Butterface ("Everything looks good on her, but her face.")

And the following terms are just plain mean:

- Bugly or Buttly (butt + ugly)
- Fugly (you can guess)
- Busted
- Brutal Alien
- Sea Donkey
- Two-bagger
- Third Place In A Hammer Fight
- Shot in the Face
- Sack of nickels (Looks like they've been hit with a...)

Rush

The process in which you shop yourself around to Greek organizations. Often fun for guys: parties, sports, guy-stuff. Usually not so fun for girls: fake conversations, skits, girly-stuff.

[Advice: Don't confuse rushing with pledging, which is when you give yourself to the Greek organization to be trained, schooled, and...well...you know. Usually not too fun for either gender.]

S

Sad Grad

What you don't want to become: an in-debt, no-job-having, living-back-with-your-P's type of person.

That homecoming party was just a bunch of Sad Grads bitching about life after school.

Sausage Party

A gathering of many more men than women. Also known as a **Sausage Fest**, **Weenie Roast, Meat Market**, or **Froman Fest** (Abe Froman "The Sausage King of Chicago" from "Ferris Bueller's Day Off").

Scout

When you have to fart really badly, but don't want to make a stink in class, so you let out a scout to test the waters.

Sentinels

People at a party who don't live there, yet patrol the party cracking down on mis-behavers despite their lack of authority to do anything about it.

Sexiled

When someone is forced to sleep outside his/her room when his/her roommate wants to have sex in the room. Also **Get the Boot**.

Shack

A verb meaning to spend the night in the room of someone of the opposite sex. Like **Hook-up**, it is an ambiguous term. Be careful how you use it.

> **"Signs of a Sexile"**
>
> You and that special someone need some special time alone. How do you warn your roommate not to come in the room? First, you need to discuss this beforehand with your roomie. Second, try one of these subtle sexiling signals:
>
> 1. Place a shoe in hallway
> 2. Hang a sock on the door
> 3. Write on you message board "SPOON" (Start Planning Other Options Now)
> 4. Let your roommate walk in and catch you in the act: it will teach them a lesson for life.
>
> Third, thank them the next day and don't let them know that their bed was involved.

Shields Up

A warning to everyone in the room to pull their shirts over their noses, in preparation for a funky-ass smell.

Shields up! I just sent some scouts out.

Shoegazer

One who looks down at his or her feet all the time. You'll see many of them during freshmen orientation.

Shotgun

1. To pound a beer by puncturing the side of the can and opening the top to make the beer spurt out in a powerful stream.
2. You call "shotgun" before a roadtrip to reserve your spot in the front passenger's seat.

Sixth Grader

A thin, wimpy little mustache that some freshmen try to grow before their hormones kick in. Named after the unfortunate peach fuzz that starts growing on 6th-grade boys. Also known as the **70's Porn Star**.

Sloppy Seconds

To have something after someone else has been there. Often used in terms of being the second person to hook up with same individual.

Sonny

An extremely good-looking male.

Serena, that guy is Sonny!

Sor-whore

A derogatory term for a member of a sorority.

Spins

This is when you are so drunk that it feels like the room won't stop spinning.

[Advice: One proven way to slow down the spins while trying to sleep is to place one foot on floor and a hand on the wall. The very best way to avoid the spins is to not drink too much in the first place.]

Stank

A bad smell. Also known as **Funk**.

Who drop da stank? My eyes are watering.

Starter Marriage Season

Refers to the numerous weddings, which take place following graduation. Many don't even last 5 years.

[Advice: When the wedding virus spreads through your posse of friends, be prepared: it comes fast and it comes with a hefty price tag. Between tux rentals, travels costs, hotels, and gifts, you'll really need to eat and drink a butt-load to break even.]

Stranger

Sitting on your hand until it becomes numb, then pleasuring yourself. It feels like someone else, "a stranger," is doing it for you.

Stranger-ette

Same as above, but paint your nails.

Suicide Break

Going outside a bar to smoke a cigarette.

Swamp Ass

A non-fatal condition in which one experiences constant intestinal distress and anal leakage. While not contagious, it does affect everyone within smelling distance.

Swayze

Someone who is exceptionally smooth, like Patrick Swayze in all his 80's flicks.

Sweater Meat

Breasts.

Sword Fight

1. Two guys getting into a heated argument but never throwing a punch.
2. Two guys pissing in the same toilet at the same time.

T

Take the kids to the pool

To poop.

Don't leave, I got to take the kids to the pool before we go.

"What's the Poop on Poop?"

We had to do it. Everyone poops and college kids all share the same potty, so it's no surprise that they've developed many names for the old #2.

A horse peaking out, Baby makes cake, Backdoor stinger, Backing out the finless brown trout, Blast a deuce, Bombs over Crapdad, Build a log cabin, Bury a Quaker, Captain's Log, Chasing ducks, Dookie Houser, Download some Software, Drop anchor, Drop the "S" bomb, Drop the Chalupa, Feed the Devil, Float a swan, Get your grumpy on, Go take a [enter someone's name], Go to the Plop Plop room, Grow a tail, Launch a sea pickle, Lay an egg, Make a doozy, Make a mud slide, Nasty Pickle, Number 3 (a combo of 1+2), Paint the White House black, Peel out, Pinch a loaf, Poop Diddy, Post a letter, Put an end to farts, Release a hostage, Send a fax, Sending the Browns to the Super Bowl, Squat a yam, Take my medication—i.e. dumpacillin, Unload cargo, Visit Dennis (Hopper), Visit from Mr. Shittz McCrappen, Zappin' Bugs

TDI

Trivial Drinking Injury usually just minor bruises, scratches or sprains.

Team Jesus

A group of fervent religious students who proselytize and preach with extreme passion and sometimes little tact. Also called the **God Squad, Holy Rollers,** and **Bible Beaters**.

Test Files

Past tests and notes kept by organizations to help their fellow members.

That Guy

An individual one does not wish to become. A social sore who decides things like exposing oneself in public or driving drunk are good ideas. Often commits party fouls. Sometimes someone's alter ego; sometimes they're just like that, all the time.

Thousand-yard stare

That glazed-over look that drunks possess when they appear to have the ability to look past people, screen doors, and bushes.

I asked if he needed a ride, but Barry just gave me the thousand-yard stare.

Three & F

Going on three dates and having sex on the third.

REAL COLLEGE MEMORY:
"Ninja Stalker Scare"

My freshman year, I was all pumped to go to this Halloween mixer with the first gal I'd gone "Three & F" with. However, Sandra decided to put me on the bus to Dumpsville a week before the big event.

I was going as a Ninja. I had bought numchuks and borrowed a way-cool black ninja costume from my bud back home. A couple of nights before the big event, I got plastered (Note: this was back in 1986 when it was still LEGAL for 18 year olds to drink alcohol) and put on the Ninja costume to practice some Drunken Fist moves. I climbed out of my 3rd floor room at Jester South and managed to fall into the bushes without any TDIs. At that point, I began stumbling through the shadows across campus making like Chuck Norris on a six-pack of Shiner Bock.

At one point, in a grove of trees just north of the Student Union, I climbed up an oak and was crouched on one of the branches, determined to pull off a cat-land. Unfortunately, my beer goggles didn't allow me to see a little bow-headed sor-whore walking down the unlit sidewalk towards the tree where I was perched.

I dropped out of the tree and landed about three feet in front of said sor-whore and shouted "HIYAAAHHH!" in a slurred voice. Sor-whore screamed at the top of her lungs: "RAAAAPE! HEEEELLLP! RAAAAPE!" She ran in one direction, while I ran in the other direction muttering to myself, "Ohshit!Ohshit!Ohshit!Ohshit!Ohshit!"

After I was halfway across campus, I took to the shadows, sobered up by adrenaline, and managed to sneak back to my room without being caught. I was lucky too, because I had a couple close calls with the Campus Police Dept. who were already combing the area looking for the alleged assailant. I finally got back to my room, tore off the costume, threw it into the bottom of the closet, jumped into bed and hid under the covers, certain that the CPD would be banging down my door any minute.

The next day, the headline of the Daily Texan read "Ninja Stalker Attacks Lone Coed." The whole campus was buzzing about the "Ninja Stalker" and I was feeling sicker and sicker as the day wore on. A couple of my buds then asked me after one of many discussions as to the Ninja Stalker's identity "Hey Sonny, weren't you going as a Ninja for Halloween?"

I quickly replied, "No! I'm going as a clown!" Then, I had to fight the urge to bang my head against the wall when two chicks started talking behind me in class saying "Ooooh! The Ninja Stalker! I bet he's cute! He probably has a nice set of numchuks and a big bo-staff!"

At the Halloween Mixer, there were tons of guys and girls dressed as Ninjas, with me as the lone clown. As luck would have it, I hooked up with this hot babe from San Antonio who was dressed like a cross between a mime and a Chinese Opera character. I guess the clown costume made me stand out!

—University of Texas-Austin

Three S's

Shit, Shower, and Shave. Part of every guy's pre-party ritual.

Three Second Rule

If a piece of food falls on the floor, one has three seconds to retrieve it before it gets too dirty to eat. Less than three seconds and the food in question is safe to ingest. A drunken version is the **Ten Second Rule**.

Throw a Haymaker

To punch with extreme force. Often used in fights to knock someone on their ass.

Throw a Haymaker

Time traveling

Used to describe periods of blackout during drinking.

I don't know how I got on the side of the highway, must have been time traveling.

Tomb of the Dead Soldiers

A trashcan filled with many, many beer cans. Sometimes brings a tear to the eye.

Towing an Anchor

When the person you want to chat up is traveling around that night with an unattractive friend. This person, the anchor, often convinces their friend, your target, that it is time to go home instead of staying with you. Also known as **FFS** (Fat Friend Syndrome), **DUFF** (Designated Ugly Fat Friend) or **Flat Tire**.

Townies

The freaky residents of the town where your school is located, who invade campus for no particularly good reason. Usually the source of good bar fights.

Transfer Disconnection

When someone transfers to another college to be with their significant other only to be dumped within three months of their arrival.

[Advice: You might feel like you can't live without your high school sweetie, but be prepared those longings in your loins might change when you get fully entrenched in the college experience.]

Travelers

Alcohol you take with you on the way to events, bars, and parties. Also known as **Road Sodas** or **Roadies.**

[Advice: Know the laws of your location—open containers are often illegal. Of course, underage drinking is ALWAYS illegal.]

Troll

A squat ugly person.

Trolling

To be scouting or passively looking for a potential hookup.

Trustafarian

A trust-fund baby that tries to act like a crunchy granola. Often try to grow white-guy dreadlocks. Very unfortunate.

Tuna Party

The female version of a **Sausage party**.

Turd Ferguson

See **That Guy**.

Two Pump Chump

A guy who climaxes very quickly.

U

UDI

Short for Unidentified Drinking Injury. This is an injury that results from a hard night of drinking. You wake up and have no idea how you hurt yourself. Whether it be a sprained ankle or cuts and bruises, you just hurt. Not to be confused with an IUD.

"What are those scratches on your butt?"

You go out. You wake up the next day. You find some weird marks on your bod. See if you can identify them.

MDA (Mysterious Drinking Accident) — The cause of a UDI

TDI (Trivial Drinking Injury) — minor bruises, scratches and sprains

SDI (Serious Drinking Injuries) — Did you have to go to a hospital?

Work of beer gnomes — The only explanation for all of the above

Ultimate

Short for Ultimate Frisbee. A game that combines Frisbee, soccer, football, and Phish fans. Often played on quads by crunchy people between drum sessions.

Upper-Decker

An act of revenge to be performed at a party where they have treated you or your friends like crap. It consists of going to the bathroom, opening the lid on the top of the toilet, taking a big crap in the water tank, and putting the lid back on. Also called **Top Shelving**.

V

V Card

Slang for virginity. One can keep it and protect or have it revoked.

REAL COLLEGE MEMORY:
"Freaky Freshman First Time"

As a commuter student, I didn't have that many on-campus contacts, especially freshman year. Unfortunately, being out of the campus picture (for me), meant being out of the pants of the girls that dwelled on campus.

At 18, I spent most of my free time chilling with my friends from high school. I was still a virgin, and absurdly thought I was going to die holding my v-card. And one day while I was wallowing in my virginity in front of my computer, somebody hit me up on AOL. This person claimed to be a girl and she liked my profile. Normally I'm wary of people I meet online, but I thought that I'd give this one a chance. This person did, in fact, turn out to be a girl. She lived in the next town over and went to a local, all-girl's private school.

That first online conversation quickly turned to things of a sexual nature and, over the next three days, we had all kinds of hanky-panky sex talk over the Net. On the morning of the fourth day, I finally garnered the nerves to ask her if she wanted to meet in person. We agreed to meet later that week at a local coffee shop, across from my campus.

I arrived a little early, and waited patiently, hoping I wouldn't be stood up. When she arrived, I was bowled over (and relieved that she showed). She was exactly as she had described herself: beautiful Korean face, black hair, about 5'3" 95 pounds, petite and hot as hell.

During our online convos, she told me that if we were ever to meet, I should say some code word to ask her to have sex in an unassuming way. To this day, I can't remember what the damn code word was. But, after three hours of coffee talk, I used it in conversation and her response: "I don't know—we'll see."

At least it wasn't a "no." We eventually decided to rent a movie and hang back at my house. While watching the movie, I made no moves whatsoever—despite the fact that I continued to be bowled over by her beauty. But about 25 minutes into the movie, SHE cozied up to ME!

Things progressed from there-from hot to heavy. It was wild. When it was over, we said goodnight. I gave her a kiss and she scurried off into the night. Then, I gunned my car at top speed to the local greasy spoon diner to find my friends and tell them all about how I lost my V-card. The next day I called the girl to see how she was doing. She told me she was having family problems and that it would be better if I didn't call her from them on. "I'll call you when things are better," she said. She never called back.

Months later I was at a party talking to some girls who went to the same school as she did. They told me that she had come down with some illness (read: STD), and that she and her family had moved to southern Ohio. I'm clean of STD's to this day. I was very sorry to hear of her health problems. Wherever you are, and you know who you are, thank you for throwing down with an unknown guy.

—John Carroll University

Vitamin N

Short for Vitamin Nicotine. Refers to having a cigarette first thing in the morning.

Vurp

When you burp but some vomit comes up too. A very nasty experience.

W

Wake and bake

The habit of starting one's morning with a toke. Also known as **Undie Bongs.**

Walk of shame

The long, humiliating walk across campus in the same thing you had on the previous night almost always involves hooking up. JBF hair and last night's clothes are dead giveaways.

REAL COLLEGE MEMORY:
"Girl Takes Walk of Shame"

I'm not sure what it is about the first few weeks of school, but everybody feels the need to just hook up like crazy.

So it was the first big night at school and everybody that I knew went to this club. My friends and I were dancing and just having a good time. And somehow, (my memory is a little unclear) I began hooking up with this guy on the dance floor. Apparently we were enjoying each other's company because we decided to go home together. For a really stupid reason, I agreed to go back to his fraternity house as opposed to my private, clean apartment. I didn't know the guy that well, so I was a little weirded out when I woke up next to him undressed, at around 6 in the morning.

I really had to pee so I put my shoes on and paraded out of his room in my little short skirt, high heels and tube top from the night before. As I stumbled back from the bathroom, I realized something, something absolutely horrifying. I had absolutely no recollection of which room in the fraternity house was his. All the rooms that could have possibly been his were locked.

There I was, stuck in the fraternity house in my little whore outfit. What was even worse is that I left my bag in his room, which had the entrance card to the gate of my apartment complex, money and my keys. Luckily, I found an open room from where I called the cab company to request an immediate pickup. Then, at the apartment complex, I had to call my roommate at 6:30

in the morning from the call box to let me in AND to pay for my cab. But, the absolute worst feeling was having to go back later that day to get my bag.

—Emory University

Walk on the Other Side of the Road

To change one's sexual preference. Also know for **Batting for the Other Team**.

Weak sausage

One who always wants to go home early just when things get interesting.

Wets

Condoms. Also known as **Hats, Jimmy Caps,** and **Raincoats**.

[Advice: Condoms are widely available on most campuses. If you think you might need one, pick them up. Don't be scared. But remember that they ain't 100% effective.]

Wife beater

A tight white undershirt worn by college males and stars of "COPS"—sleeves are optional; stains are mandatory. Can be worn under a suit-coat trying to do a "Miami Vice" retro look.

Wifed up

To be pussy-whipped. When one of your boys is missing in action, because he is spending time with his girlfriend.

Ay yo, why didn't Barry come chill wit us? Man that fool is wifed up tonight.

Wingman

A friend who helps you meet a hottie by entertaining other friends in the party. When two groups of the opposite sex meet, the wingman talks to the ugly one of the other group in order to ensure the success of the rest of one's group. Also known as **Hitman, Setting the Pick,** or **Jumping On the Grenade.**

[Advice: Thank your wingman or wingwoman. Treat them well. Buy them dinner; without their help, things can get ugly, real quick.]

Women-B-shoppin'

A single phrase that is used as a generic response for why certain females behave as they do.

Why isn't she at the party? Well just because Women-B-shoppin'!

Wounded soldier

A full beer found when cleaning up the next day after a party. Also known as **Grenade, Larry** and **Spalding** (in loving tribute to the character in "Caddyshack"). If you drink them while you clean up, you are **Bayoneting the Wounded.**

Y

Yard sale

A wipeout when one's possessions get scattered across the landscape. Often used in skiing.

When Barry slipped in the puddle with his full tray of food, it was a total yard sale.

Yef

A sarcastic remark derived from the word "yes," but meaning exactly the opposite. The opposite of Yef is **Bo**.

Is it true you hooked up with that fat townie? Uh, Yef.

[Advice: Using these opposite terms too much is guaranteed to get your ass kicked.]

YAV

Short for Yuppie Assault Vehicle. An SUV.

Yuppie Food Coupons

Reference to $20 bills. ATMs used to distribute multiple denominations, but now they only distribute 20's. Makes it hard to split the bill when a large group goes out.

Z

Za

Short for pizza.

[Advice: You can call pizza "za" but you are printing your own ticket for an ass-kicking. It's up there with calling beer "brew ha-ha."]

Zamboni

A roll of paper towels or toilet paper used to mop up spilled fluids—particularly helpful during drinking games. The roll is kept spooled and simply dragged across the spill.

Zonk

A game of dice and pot smoking. The goal being to reach 10,000 points first, but you must rely on the luck of your dice throws. Used as an excuse to get really high.

"It's Not Just for the Butt"

TP, toilet paper, toilet tissue. It doesn't matter what you call it, you'll want to keep at least one roll in your room at all times.

Here are just a few of its many uses:
- Note pad
- Napkin dispenser
- Door stop
- Streamers for party
- Mummy costume
- Cheap-o welcome banner

Zamboni

AFTERWORD

So what have we learned? Don't walk in if there's a single shoe in front of your door. A bedspring can be a scrotum's worst nightmare. And you shouldn't talk to strangers or someone while they are doing the "stranger."

But most importantly, we hope you realized how slanted and fun the world of college students really is. If you are heading away to college, we hope you learned a little about what to expect and look forward to. If you are currently a student, we hope you cherish the experience before you become a working stiff in a cube—or an unemployed stiff working on a large stuffed-crust pizza in your parents' basement. Finally, if you are like us and long to relive those salad days on campus, we hope that we offered a few chances to reflect on your own priceless college memories.

We sure did.

P.S. Don't forget to share your new terms with us at CollegeStories.com. Maybe your entries will be in our follow-up book, tentatively titled: *Too Turd, Too Ferguson.*

ABOUT THE AUTHORS

Ben Applebaum and Derrick Pittman are college friends from Wake Forest University who started CollegeStories.com in 1999.

Over the past 4 years, CollegeStories.com has grown into an underground favorite for one simple reason: it's the leading place for reveling in the college experience. Every day, thousands of undergrads, recent grads and not-so recent grads log on to read and share those defining stories from campus life. With more than 2,000 real stories and an extensive lexicon of college slang, CollegeStories.com has raised the tradition of story swapping to an art form—or as *The Tuscaloosa News* says "[their stories] read like smooth, flowing novel excerpts that could entertain even Ernest Hemingway." Who, by the way, really knew how to party.

Ben now lives in Connecticut; Derrick lives in Georgia. CollegeStories.com still lives on the web.

SHOUT-OUTS[1]

We owe the sincerest gratitude to so many who have supported us in one way or another. Recognizing you here is one small way we can show you our appreciation.

For making the book much more fun to look at: Burt Falgui for the sweet illustrations and Donald Mock for the sausagey cover art.

For publishing our asses, Jon D. McWilliams and everyone at iUniverse.

For their loving support and encouragement: Val Applebaum, Heidi Slocum, Jackie Pittman, Maggie Applebaum, Michael Pittman, Mel Applebaum, Ed Applebaum, Shelly Pittman, Jessica Janco and John Pittman.

A special thanks to the following for their ongoing support of CollegeStories.com: for his wonderful work with FilmFrat and simply for the power of Nally, Ryan McNally; for some heavy-duty creative plumbing, Steve French; and for all-around good advice, AJ Rollins.

An extra special thanks goes to our agent at Levine Greenburg, Stephanie Kip Rostan.

Props

For their various contributions to the success of CollegeStories.com and this book, we want to thank: Ashlyn Broderick, Ryan "Butta" Bifulco, Randy Zawadiuk, Jeffrey Vanderslice, Sam Fasulo, Sean Stake, Tracy Frizell, Brett Witter, Amanda Wolfe, Beau Wilberding, Brian Berklich, Brett Balsinger, Warne Fitch,

---

1. In hopes that we might score some free tickets or an on-air plug, a shout out goes to all of the great WFU b-ballers, including: Rodney Rogers, Tim Duncan, Josh Howard, Randolph Childress and of course, Mr. Bogues. Just thank "Turd Ferguson" in an interview and you'll get a free copy. Hell, that goes for anyone doing any interview.

Ross Kuhner, Mino, Chris "Alphamale" Keenan, Clive Thompson, Dan Alexander, Hank Lewis, Jason Marziotto, Jason McCann, Graham Verdon, John Cornett, Jordan Wallach, Julie Jones, Matt Bender, Paul Farris, Steve Larosiliere, Timothy Baynham, Elizabeth Silver, Jim O'Connell, Bryan Cramer, Lydia Grassi, Thomas DiFransico Jr., Boz, Joey Rahimi, Jeremy Head, Heather Harmon, Jessica Orczyk, Sean "Gill" Gillis, Jonathan Skindzier, Keg Killa, the Boys of the Fat Farm, Sarah Szefi, Zach Everson, Meredith Cummings, Luis Barreto, Marcus Sakey, Jay Wilson, PJ from OCAS, Justin Ross, Mike Maher and Doug Kelker.

A special thanks goes out to Patrick (aka Wenis) who, in many ways, was the inspiration for CollegeStories.com.

Thanks to all Demon Deacons—past and present—and to everyone from Mt. Lebanon, Lafayette, and Ridge High Schools.

**For more about this book,
visit CollegeSlang.com**

0-595-30923-2

Printed in the United States
21258LVS00004B/449